13 Paintings
Children Should Know

Angela Wenzel

PRESTEL

Munich · Berlin · London · New York

Contents

The 13 pictures you will find in this book are some of the most famous works of art of all time. They continue to fascinate people to this day—either because they remain a mystery, because they point to a new style of painting, or because they represent an accurate picture of a particular period. Let them work their spell on you too as you learn about their history and importance. The glossary at the back of the book explains the expressions which you may not know and a timeline shows you what was happening when the pictures were painted.

Tips for further reading and web addresses will help you if you want to find out more about a particular picture or artist. There are some quiz questions about what you can see in the paintings too. And last but not least, there are lots of suggestions for pictures you can paint yourself.

Have fun looking, reading, and painting!

Explanation of special words*

Artist:
  Jan van Eyck
Title:
  The Arnolfini Portrait
Painted in:
  1434
Location:
  National Gallery,
  London
Medium:
  Oil on panel
Dimensions:
  82.2 x 60 cm
Style:
  Gothic*

Love and Marriage

Here we are in the bedroom of a rich man's house in Bruges, a town in Flanders, in 1434.

What is it that we are about to see? Is the gentleman in the ermine-trimmed velvet cape and hat really Giovanni Arnolfini, a member of a wealthy Italian merchant family which also had a branch in Bruges? And is the lady in the green gown with the intricately worked sleeves his bride, Giovanna Cenami? Does the picture show their engagement or their wedding?

In those days people did not get married in a registry office or a church. They would promise to be faithful to each other in front of witnesses at home. During such a wedding ceremony the bridegroom would offer his bride his right hand. "Left-handed" or "morganatic" marriages, as they were called, only took place between a couple of unequal status. Giovanna, however, also came from a prosperous family.

Jan van Eyck, Portrait of Giovanni Arnolfini, c. 1439/40 Gemäldegalerie Berlin

Unfortunately we cannot be really sure that this painting is a portrait of Giovanni Arnolfini. Some people even think it is a self-portrait of the artist. In that case the large picture would show Jan van Eyck and his wife Margarete.

Is the gentleman in the hat perhaps Giovanni's brother Michele? We know that he fell in love with a woman called Elisabeth who, it is thought, was not as rich and grand as he was. Maybe Michele wanted to give Elisabeth this precious and elaborate picture as proof of his love and console her for the fact he could only marry her "with his left hand".

One thing is sure, however: Jan van Eyck was there! He signed* the picture as the artist and witness of the ceremony "Johannes de Eyck fuit hic 1434", he wrote above the mirror—which means: "Jan van Eyck was here, 1434."

4

What can you see in the mirror but not in the actual picture?

The mirror is a convex* mirror. Because it is curved it reflects a larger section of the room than a flat mirror, which people in van Eyck's time had not yet learned to make. You can see several people. Do you think one of them could be the artist? The pictures around the frame show the Passion of Christ and the burning candle is a symbol of Christ's presence.

Every detail, no matter how ordinary, has a symbolic meaning.

The little dog stands for a woman's faithfulness.

Is the bride expecting a baby?

Possibly, but dresses elaborately gathered at the waist were very fashionable at the time the picture was painted.

Quiz
Saint Margaret is the patron saint of mothers-to-be. Can you spot the little statue of the saint which Jan van Eyck has painted in his picture?
(Answer on page 46)

c. 1400 Rise of the Medici
1400 First excavations of ancient Rome

1434 Jan van Eyck paints *The Arnolfini Portrait*

1434–64 Cosimo de' Medici,
Ruler of Florence

1395   1400   1405   1410   1415   1420   1425   1430   1435   1440   1445   14

Artist:
  Sandro Botticelli
  (1445–1510)
Title:
  La Primavera (Spring)
Painted in:
  c. 1478
Location:
  Uffizi, Florence
Medium:
  Tempera on panel
Dimensions:
  203 x 314 cm
Style:
  Early Renaissance*

"Earth has not anything to show more fair"

Venus is the Roman goddess of beauty and love. Buds burst into flower and everything blossoms in her garden in spring. Just like in Paradise.

Venus stands in the middle of the painting framed by luxuriant orange trees. Sandro Botticelli and his contemporaries were very interested in the ancient Greeks and Romans—their philosophy, literature, and art—especially in Botticelli's native city of Florence. The city was ruled at the time by the Medici family who turned Florence into a center of the arts. Perhaps they commissioned *La Primavera* to mark the wedding of a relative, Lorenzo di Pierfrancesco. The ceremony took place on a Friday, which is called *venerdi* in Italian—the "Day of Venus."

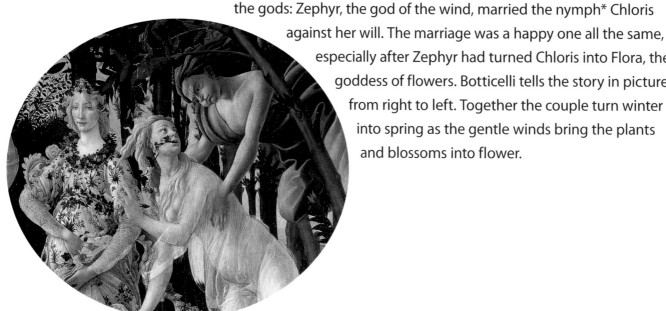

On the right in the picture there is a reference to a wedding of one of the gods: Zephyr, the god of the wind, married the nymph* Chloris against her will. The marriage was a happy one all the same, especially after Zephyr had turned Chloris into Flora, the goddess of flowers. Botticelli tells the story in pictures from right to left. Together the couple turn winter into spring as the gentle winds bring the plants and blossoms into flower.

1445–1510 Sandro Botticelli

1452–1519 Leonardo da Vinci

c. 1478 *La Primavera*

1471–1528 Albrecht Dürer

53–76 Simonetta Vespucci

1469–92 Lorenzo I de' Medici, known as Il Magnifico

53–78 Giuliano I de' Medici

(the Magnificent), Ruler of Florence

1492 Christopher Columbus discovers the New World

55   1460   1465   1470   1475   1480   1485   1490   1495   1500   1505   1510

Quiz

Like a nature studies lesson: Which of the different flowers and plants can you identify by name?

(Answer on page 46)

9

The young women in the veil-like dresses are the Three Graces* who were attendants to Venus. They represent beauty and virtue—qualities which a bride was expected to possess. On the far left, Mercury is driving away the dark clouds which must not be allowed to obscure the future.

Mercury is the god of trading and merchants—possibly a reference to the Medici, who had made their fortune as bankers.

Cupid, the god of love and the son of Venus and Mercury, hovers above the scene. He is aiming his arrow right at the heart so that his "victim" will fall in love immediately.

Sandro Botticelli,
Simonetta Vespucci,
c. 1480-85
Gemäldegalerie Berlin

How alike they are! This portrait by Botticelli shows Simonetta Vespucci, who was thought to be the most beautiful woman in Florence. She was the mistress of Giuliano de' Medici, Cosimo's grandson. Unfortunately Simonetta died when she was only 23. Botticelli worshipped Simonetta and wanted to be buried at her feet after his death. Simonetta was probably the model he used for the figure of Flora. The Florentine lady was not just known for her beauty but also for her intelligence and elegance.

How would you paint a picture of spring?

You can find more information about the *Mona Lisa* on the web page www.schools-wikipedia.org/wp/m/Mona_Lisa.htm
At www.citesciences.fr/francais/ala_cite/expo/explora/image/mona/en.php you can change Mona Lisa's expression by mouseclick.

1503–06 *Mona Lisa*

1471–1528 Albrecht Dürer

1483–1520 Raphael
1492 Christopher Columbus discovers the New World

c. 1518 Invention of the first spectacles
for short-sightedness

180   1485   1490   1495   1500   1505   1510   1515   1520   1525   1530   1535

Why are you smiling, Mona Lisa?

Poets, singers, scientists, and artists have all come up with answers to the Mona Lisa's mysterious smile. But so far she hasn't let on to anybody.

The mystery lady is probably a portrait of the wife of Francesco del Giocondo, a Florentine merchant. That is why she is also known as "La Gioconda." She gently gazes at you, regardless of which side you approach her from. Leonardo painted her skin in indescribably delicate, shimmering hues. The landscape behind her fades into a fine veil of mist. This comes from Leonardo's special painting technique, called *sfumato*, which means "turned into smoke" or "hazy."

The *Mona Lisa* became the most famous painting in the world in 1911, when Vincenzo Peruggia, an Italian workman who was supposed to carry out some work in the Louvre, made off with the picture. It was not until two years later that it was tracked down. Today the mysterious beauty is back in the museum in Paris, but behind bullet-proof glass, where she casts her spell over millions of visitors.

If you photocopy the picture you could create your own variation on the Mona Lisa by drawing on it or turning it into a collage. Or perhaps you would simply rather paint your own version of the Mona Lisa?

Artist:
Leonardo da Vinci (1452–1519)
Title:
Mona Lisa
Painted in:
1503–06
Location:
Louvre, Paris
Medium:
Oil on poplar panel
Dimensions:
77 x 53 cm
Style:
Renaissance*

Sfumato

Leonardo used muted colors mixed with white, placing several layers of translucent glaze* on top of each other and shading the contours of the individual shapes with a paintbrush so that they appear blurred.

13

1445–1510 Sandro Botticelli

1471–1528 Albrecht Dürer

1452–1519 Leonardo da Vinci

1452 Completion of Nuremberg city wall

1492 Christopher Columbus discovers America

1440   1445   1450   1455   1460   1465   1470   1475   1480   1485   1490   1

1502

"Tell us a story!" said the March Hare

Everybody recognizes this young hare immediately! He is known as "Dürer's Hare" and pops up everywhere, especially at Easter—on serviettes, postcards, and even made of chocolate.

Artist:
  Albrecht Dürer
  (1471–1528)
Title:
  The Hare
Painted in:
  1502
Location:
  Albertina, Vienna
Medium:
  Watercolor* and
  body color on paper
Dimensions:
  25.1 x 22.6 cm
Style: Renaissance*

This animal study has been copied countless times by other artists—it is simply a perfect picture of a hare! It really looks as if it is alive although Albrecht Dürer probably painted it from a stuffed animal or perhaps even from memory. Dürer had great powers of observation and he studied nature very closely. And he was also a master of the art of painting. Wouldn't you love to stroke the hare's fur? He looks so soft and cuddly!

First of all, Dürer used watercolors* which are slightly transparent to sketch the basic shape of the body. Then, with the fine point of a paintbrush and opaque colors, he added the individual hairs in various different shades, so that finally he had created an impression of shining fur.

Dürer's *Hare* is one of the first animals to appear on its own as the subject of a picture. In Dürer's day many artists were interested in portraying nature—plants, animals, and landscapes. But no one could draw them as precisely as Albrecht Dürer. And no one else was such a master of the technique of painting with watercolor and body color. His monogram* and the year prove that he intended the picture of the hare to be seen as a work of art in its own right. You could almost call it a portrait of a hare.

Part of a window frame is reflected in the hare's eye.

Maybe Dürer was painting a live pet after all.

Albrecht Dürer, The Holy Family with Three Hares, c. 1497
Woodcut

In this picture the animals are of secondary importance or are a symbol*: in the Middle Ages the hare stood for Christ's resurrection. It can also be seen as a reference to the Trinity*.

Albrecht Dürer,
Wing of a Roller, **1512**
Watercolor and body
color
Albertina, Vienna

Nowadays rollers are
very rare birds. In Dürer's
time they were sold
in his home town of
Nuremberg as a delicacy.

Albrecht Dürer,
The Great Piece of Turf,
1503
Watercolor and body
color

Dürer was even interested
in turning something as
commonplace as a piece
of turf into a subject for
a painting. He looked at
it very closely: yarrow,
dandelion, bluegrass, and
plantain. They are not
growing at random, as
they might be in real life,
but have been positioned
carefully. The finely drawn
grasses in front make it
possible for us to see the
plantain behind as well.
The long stalks of the
dandelion and the grasses
form the background.

Between Heaven and Earth

Do you have the feeling you have seen those two little angels at the bottom of the picture somewhere before? No wonder!

For more than a century the angels have been making appearances on Advent calendars and wrapping paper, cups and napkins, table mats and tea tins, T-shirts and umbrellas. Really they don't belong there at all. They belong on this painting by the Italian artist Raphael! As putti*, gazing up at the Virgin Mary holding the Infant Jesus, they no longer look so cheeky and bored. Raphael painted the picture for the high altar of the monastery church of San Sisto in Piacenza in Italy.

Saint Barbara and Saint Sixtus, whose bones are preserved in San Sisto, are kneeling to the right and left of the Virgin. This encounter did not take place on Earth but in Heaven. Saint Sixtus is pointing at something outside the picture, and the Madonna and Child are looking in the same direction. In the church there was a crucifix hanging opposite the picture. And so Saint Sixtus was pointing at the crucified Christ and the Virgin and baby Jesus were looking at him too.

Artist:
Raphael (1483–1520)
Title:
Sixtine Madonna
Painted in:
1512/13
Location:
Gemäldegalerie
Alte Meister, Dresden
Medium:
Oil on canvas
Dimensions:
265 x 196 cm
Style: Renaissance*

Quiz
Why is the picture called the *Sixtine Madonna*?
(Answer on page 46)

Tip
Where would you like to see the angels? You can draw them onto one of your photos (or a picture taken from a magazine), or make a photocopy and stick them on.

For more than 250 years the painting has not been in its original location. In 1754 the altar came into the possession of the Elector of Saxony. Today you can see it in the Gemäldegalerie Alte Meister (Old Masters' Gallery) in Dresden.

The Papal Crown

Saint Sixtus has humbly removed his crown-like hat, known as a papal tiara (bottom left). He was elected Pope as Sixtus II in 257 and died a martyr* in 258.

Saint Barbara

Saint Barbara is kneeling beside the Madonna. At one point she was imprisoned in the tower rising up behind her.

The grace and beauty of the Madonna

and her gentle, melan-
cholic gaze were much
admired by famous
poets. If you look closely,
what appear at a distance
to be clouds turn out
to be a host of angel's
heads.

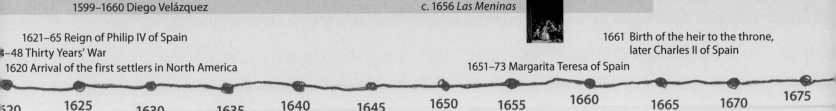

1599–1660 Diego Velázquez
c. 1656 *Las Meninas*

1621–65 Reign of Philip IV of Spain
1661 Birth of the heir to the throne, later Charles II of Spain

–48 Thirty Years' War
1620 Arrival of the first settlers in North America
1651–73 Margarita Teresa of Spain

520   1625   1630   1635   1640   1645   1650   1655   1660   1665   1670   1675

Life at Court

A scene in the studio of the Spanish court painter Diego Velázquez: He is hard at work. The rooms where he worked were in the Royal Palace in Madrid during the reign of King Philip IV.

Velázquez is using all his skill. He seems to have captured a fleeting moment, but everything in the picture has been very carefully planned. The position of the people, the effect of light and shade, the depiction of the room which draws your gaze through the open door into the depths of the picture.

The main person appears to be the little blond girl in the light-colored dress. It is Margarita, King Philip's youngest daughter. She is surrounded by her maids of honor and two people of small stature, the court dwarfs, who lived in the palace and who entertained the royal family. Why is the group positioned so far forward, as if on a stage? Who are the artist and Margarita looking at? Which picture is Velázquez working on at the moment? These are questions which are impossible to answer with any certainty. Perhaps they are looking at the King and Queen, whom we can recognise in the mirror in the background? Is the royal couple perhaps sitting for the artist so that he can paint their portrait?

Or is it the painting *Las Meninas* itself which is on the easel? Have they all taken up their positions in front of a huge mirror which Velázquez is looking into in order to paint the picture?

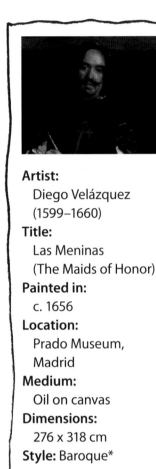

Artist:
  Diego Velázquez
  (1599–1660)
Title:
  Las Meninas
  (The Maids of Honor)
Painted in:
  c. 1656
Location:
  Prado Museum,
  Madrid
Medium:
  Oil on canvas
Dimensions:
  276 x 318 cm
Style: Baroque*

Royal Honor

In Velázquez' time painting was regarded as a craft, not as art. Nonetheless, Velázquez seems to have been very self-confident. Philip IV honored him for his achievements with a knighthood. After the artist's death it is said that the king himself painted the sign of honor onto Velázquez's chest in the painting, because the picture was completed before the artist had been awarded the title.

This valet's

job consisted of opening the door for the king.

"Mirror, mirror on the wall …"

Is it a mirror in the frame that shows a reflection of Philip IV and his consort Maria Anna of Austria? Or is it a painting like the other pictures on the walls of the room?

The Privilege of Fools

On the right-hand side of the picture we can see two court dwarfs. It is no coincidence that the dog is lying beside them: The little people didn't have to follow the social rules of behaviour but they were often treated no better than the family pets.

Try painting or drawing Margarita in modern clothes?

that Margarita was only five years old in this picture? Do you think it was possible to play in such an elegant dress? The little princess was seldom allowed to do as she pleased. There were very strict rules governing behavior at the Spanish court.

1775–1875 Joseph Mallord William (J.M.W.) Turner

1769 James Watt develops an efficient steam engine

1802 Maiden voyage of the first steam-powered tug boat

1802 First steam-powered railway engine

1805 Battle of Trafalgar

| 1760 | 1765 | 1770 | 1775 | 1780 | 1785 | 1790 | 1795 | 1800 | 1805 | 1810 |

Artist:
J.M.W. Turner
(1775–1875)
Title:
The Fighting
Téméraire
Painted in:
1839
Location:
National Gallery,
London
Medium:
Oil on canvas
Dimensions:
90.7 x 121.6 cm
Style: Romanticism*

The Greatest Painting in the United Kingdom

In a survey by the National Gallery in London and the BBC *The Fighting Téméraire* was voted the best and most famous painting in the entire country.

Both the painter and the subject are equally famous: Joseph Mallord William Turner and the "Téméraire," which means "bold."

The warship Téméraire experienced its moment of glory during the Battle of Trafalgar in 1805, which was fought between the United Kingdom on one side and the allied navies of France and Spain on the other. The Téméraire came to the assistance of the ship of the British naval commander, Lord Nelson, when the latter was under heavy fire.

Nelson himself was killed by a French rifleman, but the United Kingdom was nonetheless victorious and became the world's leading naval power.

33 years later the ancient sailing ship was towed up the Thames by modern steamships to be broken up. Turner depicted the Téméraire in a dignified white and gold of victory rather than in the colors with which it had actually been painted. It gleams like an apparition from another world behind the dark little tug.

Spectacular display

The glowing colors of the setting sun create a magnificent setting to celebrate the Téméraire.

The sails are furled

Instead of the victorious Union Jack* a white flag flutters in the breeze—a symbol of surrender.

1838 The Téméraire is sent to the scrapyard

1839 *The Fighting Téméraire*

finally defeated in the Battle of Waterloo

1826 Joseph Nicéphore Nièpce takes the first photograph

1851 First World Exhibition* in London

20   1825   1830   1835   1840   1845   1850   1855   1860   1865   1870   1875

In spite of his sadness at the end of the Téméraire and the age of sailing ships, Turner was interested in modern inventions. The smoke and sparks coming from the tug's funnel gave him an opportunity to use his special painting technique. Turner applied the oil paint in some cases as a layered glaze* like watercolors*. And then he added impastoed* thick brushstrokes of color on top.

In Turner's painting the Téméraire almost looks like a ghost ship. How about trying to paint a magnificent ship yourself?

1853–90 Vincent van Gogh

1775–1851 J. M. William Turner

1840–1926 Claude Monet

1870–71 Franco-Prussian War

1879 Thomas Alva Edison develops the light bulb

1825   1830   1835   1840   1845   1850   1855   1860   1865   1870   1875   1

What a Night!

The heavens and the stars are all worked up. Do you think that is how the artist felt deep down inside?

Artist:
Vincent van Gogh (1853–90)
Title:
The Starry Night
Painted in:
1889
Location:
Museum of Modern Art, New York
Medium:
Oil on canvas
Dimensions:
73.7 x 92.1 cm
Style:
Early Expressionism*

In his works Vincent van Gogh wanted to express his innermost feelings, which often overwhelmed him. Here they can be seen especially in the flowing forms and the impastoed*, violent brushstrokes.

Unlike many of his other paintings, van Gogh did not paint this particular one outside in the open air. He was mentally ill and was having treatment in a psychiatric hospital in the Provence region of southern France. But while he was working on the painting he must have been thinking about the velvety southern sky with its twinkling stars. Tall cypress trees also grow in this area. The village, on the other hand, looks more like van Gogh's native Holland.

The Starry Night is one of van Gogh's most famous paintings. Poems were written about it and the title is mentioned in the pop song "Vincent" by the American singer Don McLean, which is dedicated to the painter.

The artist

has applied the paint really thickly. Van Gogh is famous for his expressive* brush work.

Suggestions for further reading
Visiting Vincent van Gogh by Caroline Breunesse (in Prestel's Adventures in Art series); *Vincent van Gogh* (in Prestel's "Minis" series)

1840–1926 Claude Monet

1853–1926 Vincent van Gogh

1881–1973 Pablo Picasso

1901 *Child with a Dove*

1882–1967 Edward Hopper

1907–54 Frida Kahlo

1912–56 Jackson Pollock

1914–18 First World War

1875   1880   1885   1890   1895   1900   1905   1910   1915   1920   1925   1

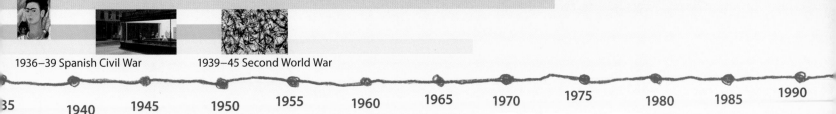
All Creatures Great and Small

Do you think the little girl is sad? She looks shy, almost frightened standing there.

Next to the child there is a ball which she doesn't pay any attention to. Perhaps she wants to protect the dove. Or does she want the bird to protect her? The little girl's dress is white and so is the dove: white is the color of innocence and purity. Lots of people love the painting because they see it as a joyful picture of peace and hope.

Children and doves play an important part in Picasso's pictures. The artist himself wanted to see the world with the eyes of a child—curious and unprejudiced. Like this little girl, the young people we come across in his works are often not meant to be a particular person. Of course Picasso often painted his own children as well: His sons Paul and Claude and his daughter. Incidentally Picasso called her Paloma, which is the Spanish word for a dove.

Artist:
Pablo Picasso
(1881–1973)
Title:
Child with a Dove
Painted in:
1901
Location:
National Gallery,
London
Medium:
Oil on canvas
Dimensions:
73 x 54 cm
Style:
Picasso's Blue Period

Pablo Picasso, The Dove, 1949, lithograph

This dove by Picasso was seen throughout the entire world as a sign of longing for and working toward peace.

A suggestion for further reading
A Day with Picasso by Susanne Pfleger (in Prestel's Adventures in Art series)

Have you got a digital camera with a zoom? If so, you can take wonderful water pictures even of a puddle. Watch how the colors and light change depending on the weather and the time of day. Perhaps your photos will give you some ideas for your own paintings.

1893 Monet lays out his water garden   c. 1915 *Water Lilies*
1914–18 First World War
1881–1973 Pablo Picasso
1882–1967 Edward Hopper
1889 Completion of the Eiffel Tower for the World Exhibition* in Paris, introduction of the first hardy colored water lilies

80   1885   1890   1895   1900   1905   1910   1915   1920   1925   1930   1935

Multicolored Water Lilies

In the garden which he created near Paris Monet found some of his favorite picture motifs, including this water landscape with water lilies.

Until 1875 there were no water lilies in Europe with colored petals like those Monet has painted here. Before that, only white water lilies grew in these latitudes, because they were the only ones which were frost-resistant. That was until the gardener Joseph Bory Latour-Marliac crossed them with exotic waterlilies. The new, hardy varieties were pink, yellow and dark red and they were presented to the general public for the first time at the World Exhibition* in 1889.

Claude Monet was fascinated. He created a water garden especially for these beautiful plants in Giverny near Paris. As a painter he was not interested in the botanical details but in the colorful impression of the blossoms and leaves and the reflections of the sky and the banks in the water. That is why he only showed a section of the pool surface and nothing else. In order to record the changing light reflections and colors he painted the water lilies at all times of day, and even at night.

Color mosaic

The fleeting reflections of light and the shapes on the surface of the water allowed Monet great artistic freedom.
The objects disintegrate and become colored dots, lines, and surfaces.

Artist:
Claude Monet (1840–1926)
Title:
Water Lilies
Painted in:
c. 1915
Location:
Neue Pinakothek, Munich
Medium:
Oil on canvas
Dimensions:
140 x 185 cm
Style: Impressionism*

Tip
In Giverny, some 80 km (50 miles) west of Paris you can still visit and admire Monet's garden with the water lilies in all their glory.
In the Musée de l'Orangerie in Paris you can immerse yourself in Monet's world of colors. There you will find eight enormous water lily pictures which completely cover the walls of two oval rooms.

1881–1973 Pablo Picasso

1882–1967 Edward Hopper

1907–54 Frida Kahlo

1912–56 Jackson Pollock

1914–18 First World War

1875   1880   1885   1890   1895   1900   1905   1910   1915   1920   1925

A Double Portrait

The Mexican artist Frida Kahlo was as beautiful and proud as she has shown herself in this portrait.

She looks at us seriously and questioningly. She must have looked just as intensely at herself in the mirror when she painted this picture. Frida Kahlo did not have an easy life. As a child she suffered from polio and when she was 18 she broke her spine in a traffic accident. Afterwards she was in constant pain.

Her companion, by contrast, the little monkey, is a merry, comical creature. He almost looks human. Perhaps he represents the other, cheerful side of Frida Kahlo, who could also be full of the joys of life. Behind them you can see the fleshy leaves of the exotic plants which grew in the artist's garden. She loved animals and kept parrots and dogs belonging to an old pre-Colombian race. She also painted a picture of herself with them.

Artist:
Frida Kahlo (1907—54)
Title:
Self-Portrait with Monkey
Painted in:
1938
Location:
Albright-Knox Art Gallery, Buffalo
Medium:
Oil on hardboard
Dimensions:
40.6 x 30.5 cm
Style:
Surrealism*

Tip
Under http://fkahlo.com you will find lots of pictures and photos of and by Frida Kahlo together with information about her in English and Spanish.

A suggestion for further reading
Frida Kahlo: The Artist in the Blue House by Magdalena Holzhey (in Prestel's Adventures in Art series)

How about trying to paint a double portrait of yourself with your favorite animal?

The colors of the 1940s

Hopper blends the broken* and yet luminous colors with great skill and feeling.

1942 *Nighthawks*

1907–54 Frida Kahlo

1912–56 Jackson Pollock

1939–45 Second World War

es enter the First World War   1926 The fluorescent tube is invented   1938 Commercial distribution of fluorescent tubes begins

930   1935   1940   1945   1950   1955   1960   1965   1970   1975   1980   1985

Strangers in the Night

Just like a film! It looks as if Humphrey Bogart alias detective Philip Marlowe might come round the corner any minute …

It is late at night; the streets are deserted. All sorts of dangers may be lurking in the shadows. The restaurant, as bright as a lightship, is on a dark street corner. Does it really offer any shelter? The guests are lost in thought, isolated, alone, while the barman carries on with his work. The fluorescent lighting, which was becoming more and more popular at the time, is eerie and hard. It contrasts strongly with the dark shadows and heightens the feeling of menace and despair.

Edward Hopper was inspired to paint this picture by a restaurant, long since gone, which used to stand at a junction on Greenwich Avenue in New York. The glass shopfront is typical of the architecture of the Art Déco* period. The guests are dressed in the fashion of the times. It must have looked very like this in New York during the 1940s. But lonely people in big cities today still probably feel very like the "nighthawks" in this picture.

Just imagine what a thrilling short story you could write about this painting!

Artist:
Edward Hopper (1882–1967)
Title:
Nighthawks
Painted in:
1942
Location:
The Art Institute of Chicago
Medium:
Oil on canvas
Dimensions:
84.1 x 152.4 cm
Style:
American Realism*

Tip
In Prestel's *Coloring Book: Edward Hopper* you will find more pictures by Hopper to color and complete!

A suggestion for further reading
Edward Hopper: Summer at the Seashore by Deborah Lyons (in Prestel's Adventures in Art series)

Quiz
What an unusual shape
the picture has! What
does it remind you of?

(Answer on page 46)

1912–56 Jackson Pollock

1950 *Number 32*

1907–54 Frida Kahlo

1917 The United States enter the First World War

1945 The United Stat

1914–18 First World War

1941 The United States enter the Second World

1900   1905   1910   1915   1920   1925   1930   1935   1940   1945   1950   1

Artist:
  Jackson Pollock
  (1912–56)
Title:
  Number 32
Painted in:
  1950
Location:
  K20K21
  Kunstsammlung
  Nordrhein-Westfalen,
  Düsseldorf
Medium:
  Gloss paint on
  canvas
Dimensions:
  269 x 457.5 cm
Style:
  Abstract
  Expressionism*

Once Upon a Time in America

Humongous and covered with splashes of paint—and
nothing else!

Modern times call for new subjects and innovative techniques, said
American artist Jackson Pollock in the mid-1940s. He abandoned all the
old rules of painting. He didn't paint, he dripped and poured the color
onto his canvas using paintbrushes and sticks. Mostly, as in *No. 32*, he
didn't use thick oil paint but chose thin car paint instead, which he found
more suitable. All parts of the picture are equally important; there is no
center. Pollock always kept an eye on the edges of his paintings, but in fact
the web of color could be continued indefinitely.

Pollock used his "Drip Paintings" to express his innermost thoughts. They
aroused tremendous interest in both America und Europe: New York
became the new center of the art world and Pollock became a star. The
artist who took the liberty of creating pictures like this was a hero of Free
America, which in those days was the role model for the whole of the
Western world. The hero met a tragic end. Jackson Pollock had not painted
any more pictures for two whole years when, at the age of 44, he crashed
his car into a tree while under the influence of alcohol.

You can also try out Jackson Pollock's drip technique using paint on packing paper.
First cover the floor with plastic sheeting which is at least 80 cm bigger than the area
to be painted on all sides. Use no more than three colors, one of which should be black.
Instead of using a brush or stick you can also dribble the color onto the paper using an
empty tin. Jackson Pollock wrote the following instructions: "Tie an empty tin to a one
or two-meter long piece of string and bore a small hole in the bottom. Fill the tin with
liquid paint." (Before pouring in the paint you should block the hole in the tin with a
piece of modelling clay.)

1963 Assassination of U.S. President John F. Kennedy
1964–73 The United States take part in the Vietnam War
to surrender by dropping two atomic bombs on Hiroshima and Nagasaki on August 6 and 9
1961 The Berlin Wall is built

2008 Barack Obama elected 44th President
of the United States

60   1965   1970   1975   1980   1985   1990   1995   2000   2005   2010   2015

Jackson Pollock
at work

Pollock put his pictures on the floor to paint them. Then he could walk round the canvas and throw paint at it from all sides. When he was working he needed to use his entire body and to concentrate completely. The artist was, so to speak, in action, so this type of art came to be known as Action Painting.

Tip
You can also try out drip paintings in the internet under www.jacksonpollock.org

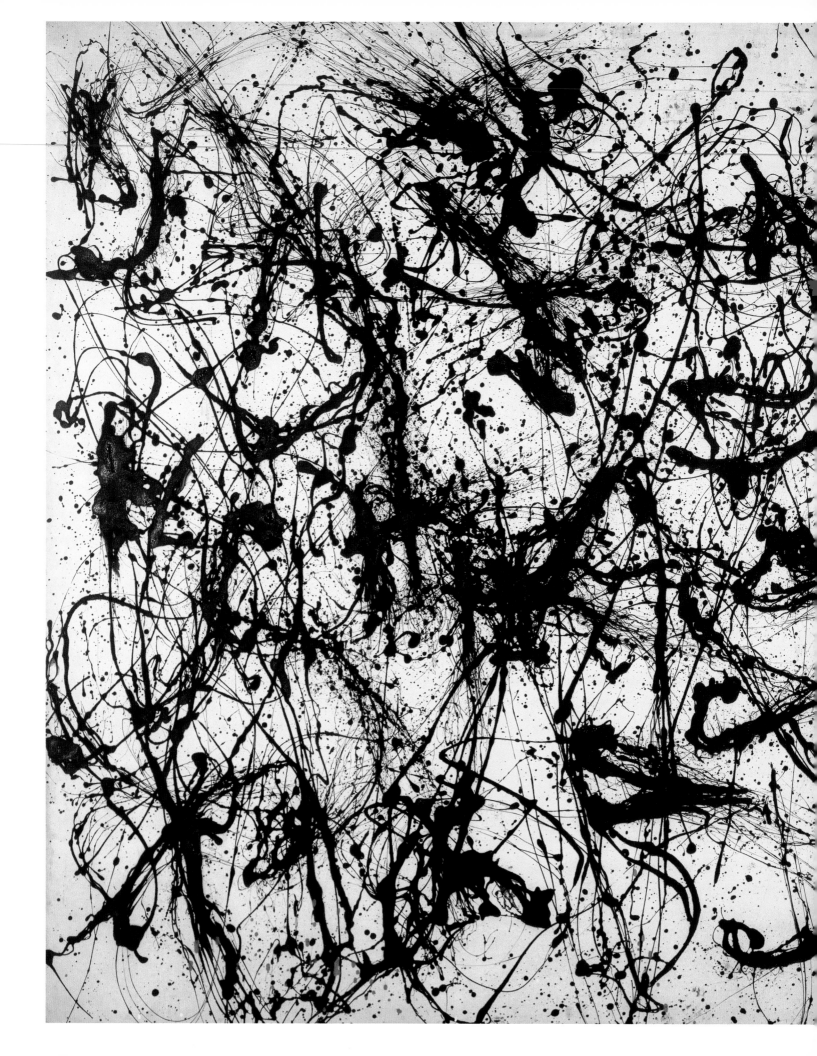

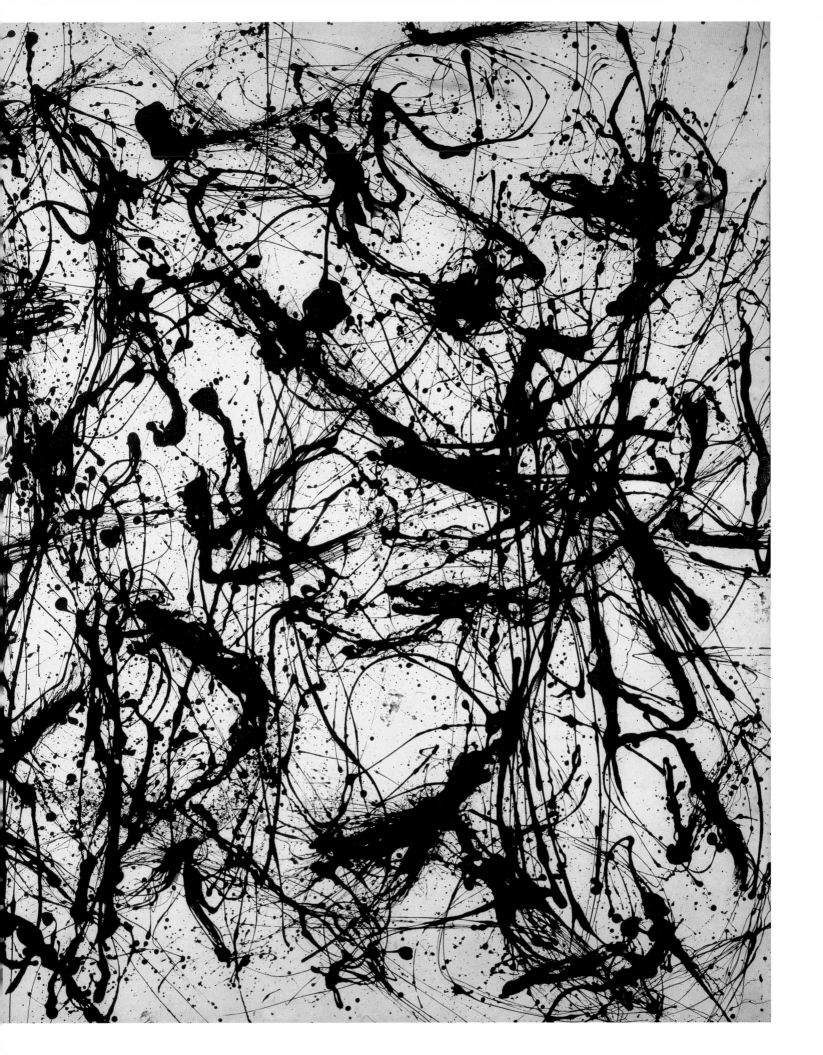

Glossary

ABSTRACT EXPRESSIONISM As in Expressionism* the painter expresses his feelings and his subconscious thoughts. However, he does not paint people or things but abstract forms which do not directly represent a specific object. The picture surface becomes a stage on which the artist goes into action. This type of art was developed in New York during the 1940s and was later also adopted in Europe.

AMERICAN REALISM This style of art developed during the early 20th century in the United States and took as its subject the reality of American life.

ART DÉCO A style in applied arts and architecture during the 1920s and 1930s. The name is an abbreviation of the French expression "arts décoratifs," meaning "decorative arts."

BAROQUE The Baroque era lasted from about 1600 until the mid-18th century. The artists were fond of curving forms full of movement. The name "Baroque" comes from the Portuguese word "barocco," which refers to an irregularly shaped, roundish pearl.

BROKEN COLORS are not pure, luminous colors. They are formed by mixing a pure color with one or more other color(s) or with black. Broken colors generally shimmer less strongly than pure colors.

CONVEX MIRROR is a mirror which curves outward at the middle. You can see more in it than in a flat mirror. For that reason convex mirrors are often positioned at road junctions where it is difficult to see the traffic.

EARLY EXPRESSIONISM
See Expressionism

EARLY RENAISSANCE
See Renaissance

EXPRESSIONISM This name was first used in 1911. Expressionist painting does not portray the actual appearance of things: artists wanted to "express" the very heart of things or their attitude to them. That is why they changed the shapes and used intense colors—as Vincent van Gogh had done before them. Important Expressionists include the painters of the "Brücke" artists's association, which was formed in Dresden, Germany, in 1905, and the members of the group "Der Blaue Reiter" (The Blue Rider), which was established in Munich in 1911.

EXPRESSIVE Full of expression.

GOTHIC A style in medieval art dating from the middle of the 12th century. The Gothic style continued until it was replaced in the 15th century, initially in Italy, by the Renaissance style. Generally speaking, Gothic painting dealt with religious subjects and not visible reality. However Jan van Eyck, who mostly painted religious works, was also a masterly observer of nature.

GRACES The goddesses of grace and Venus' attendants.

GLAZE Glaze is a thin layer of paint which lets the support (backing material) shine through. If you apply several layers the bottom ones will still shine through. All the layers combine to produce the final color. Some types of paint are especially suitable for glazing.

IMPRESSIONISM is a style of painting which developed in France between 1860 and 1870 and had a tremendous influence on the art world. It owes its name to Claude Monet's painting *Impression*. The Impressionists created personal "impressions" of what they had seen in the form of shimmering dots of light and color. They especially liked working in the open air, because there the lighting and colors changed constantly according to the time of day or the season.

IMPASTO Paint applied in thick layers.

MARTYRS People who die for their religious faith.

 **MONOGRAM** A type of signature consisting of a person's initials (from the first and family names).

NYMPH In Ancient Greek mythology, a female nature deity. Nymphs may live in the sea, in springs, streams, on mountains, in trees, and in forests.

PUTTI Cherubs. "Putto" is Italian and means "little boy."

RENAISSANCE The word comes from the French and means "rebirth." During the Renaissance, which lasted from the first half of the 15th century until about 1600, Antiquity was rediscovered as a period during which people had already displayed a great interest in the world.

ROMANTICISM Romanticism came about at the end of the 18th century and continued until well into the 19th century. It focused on the emotions as well as on the mysterious, the gruesome, and the fantastic.

SIGN To write your name.

SURREALISM The Surrealists were interested in everything which extended "beyond reality"—in French, "sur" means "over" or "above." The expression was used for the first time in 1917, and in the 1920s and 1930s the writers and artists of the Surrealist movement attracted a great deal of attention. Familiar objects were presented in an unfamiliar manner and linked together to form highly surprising and mysterious pictures rather like a dream. For the Surrealists the miraculous, the mysterious, and the surreal were all just as real as everyday reality.

SYMBOL A symbol is a sign which expresses the essential nature of an object.

TRINITY In Christian theology the Trinity stands for God the Father, his Son Jesus Christ, and the Holy Ghost.

UNION JACK The flag of the United Kingdom.

WATERCOLOR PAINT is water-soluble and can be diluted with water. It contains a very high proportion of fine pigment (colorant) and uses natural gum as a binder. Watercolors are not opaque, but the "support"—usually special white paper—shimmers through and gives the painting a special glow.

WORLD EXHIBITION is an international exhibition in which the participating countries present themselves and their achievements in technology, industry, and crafts.

Answers to the quiz:

Page 7:   In the background on the right, level with the bride's head, you can make out a carved statue of Saint Margaret.

Page 9:   Apart from the orange trees, there are roses, irises, periwinkles, myrtle, cornflowers, carnations, wild strawberries, buttercups, scarlet poppies, flax, asters, watercress, violets, and many other species of plants. A scientist at the University of Florence identified 190 different species of plants and flowers!

Page 19:   The name comes from Saint Sixtus.

Page 39:   The broad format of the picture resembles a cinema screen.

Library of Congress Control Number: 2009928581; British Library Cataloguing-in-Publication Data: a catalogue record for this book is available from the British Library; Deutsche Nationalbibliothek holds a record of this publication in the Deutsche Nationalbibliografie; detailed bibliographical data can be found under: http://dnb.ddb.de

© Prestel Verlag, Munich · Berlin · London · New York 2009

© for the illustrated works by Frida Kahlo: Banco de México Diego Rivera & Frida Kahlo Museums Trust/ VG Bild-Kunst, Bonn 2009; Pablo Picasso: Succession Picasso/VG Bild-Kunst, Bonn 2009; Jackson Pollock: Pollock-Krasner Foundation/VG Bild-Kunst, Bonn 2009; Edward Hopper, *Nighthawks*: The Art Institute of Chicago, 2009

Picture credits: Akg: Van Eyck, *The Arnolfini Portrait*; Velázquez, *Las Meninas*; Monet, *Water Lilies*; Kunstsammlung Nordrhein-Westfalen, Foto Walter Klein: Pollock, *No. 32*; The Art Institute of Chicago: Hopper, *Nighthawks*

Portraits: Jan van Eyck: *Probable Self-Portrait: Man in a Red Turban*, 1433, National Gallery, London; Leonardo da Vinci: *Self-Portrait*, c. 1516, Biblioteca Reale, Turin; Sandro Botticelli: *Self-Portrait* (Detail from the *Adoration of the Magi*), c. 1477/78, Uffizi, Florence; Raphael: *Self-Portrait* (detail), 1509, Uffizi, Florence; Albrecht Dürer: *Self-Portrait as a Boy*, 1484, Albertina, Vienna; William Turner: *Self-Portrait*, c. 1799, Tate Gallery, London; Claude Monet: Photograph, December 1899; Vincent van Gogh: *Self-Portrait with Bandaged Ear* (detail), 1889, Courtauld Art Institute Galleries, London; Pablo Picasso: Photograph; Edward Hopper: Hopper in Cape Elizabeth, Maine, Photograph 1927; Jackson Pollock: The artist in his studio, photograph

Prestel books are available worldwide. Please contact your nearest bookseller or one of the following addresses for information concerning your local distributor.

Prestel Verlag
Königinstrasse 9, 80539 Munich
Tel. +49 (0)89 24 29 08-300
Fax +49 (0)89 24 29 08-335
www.prestel.de

Prestel Publishing Ltd.
4, Bloomsbury Place, London WC1A 2QA
Tel. +44 (0)20 73 23-50 04
Fax +44 (0)20 76 36-80 04

Prestel Publishing
900 Broadway, Suite 603, New York, NY 10003
Tel. +1 (212) 995-27 20; Fax +1 (212) 995-27 33
www.prestel.com

Project management: Doris Kutschbach
Design: Michael Schmölzl, agenten.und.freunde, Munich
Translation: Jane Michael, Munich
Copyediting: Christopher Wynne, Bad Tölz
Origination: ReproLine Mediateam, Munich
Production: Nele Krüger
Printing and Binding: Tlačiarne BB, spol. s r. o.

Printed in the Slovak Republic on acid-free paper
ISBN 978-3-7913-4323-5